Introducti

Once you get into Parchment Craft, you soon want to master that fabulous lacework which parchers so often use to frame their artwork. Done traditionally, this requires lots of counting (and focus!), but Tina has developed a brilliant series of Border Pattern Grids, both straight and diagonal, to help you create beautiful gridwork and lacework easily.

Previously, we published a series of Tina Cox's *Parchment Perforating Guides*, written to accompany her clever and innovative *Border Pattern Grids*. The first books cover the basics of creating patterns using the straight and diagonal grids. Be sure to check out the *'Parchment Perforating Guide - Diagonal Border Pattern Grid No1'* (ACC-BO-30527-XX) before progressing to this book. It's not a strict necessity to do so, but I'd recommend it.

In this *ADVANCED GUIDE,* we introduce the technique of picot cutting the perforations you can make with the diagonal grid. Without too much trouble, and with the help of the grid patterns as a guide, you too will be creating masterful intricate lacework with relative ease!

Enjoy the picot trail!
Barbara Gray

Tools & Items Used In This Book

Clarity Lightwave (ACC-LP-30352-A4)
Regular parchment paper (GRO-AC-40020-A5)
Purple parchment paper (GRO-AC-40189-A5)
Blue parchment paper (GRO-AC-40190-A5)
A4 Translucent Piercing Mat (GRO-AC-40307-A4)
A4 Translucent White Super Foam (GRO-AC-40603-A4)
Pergamano Excellent Embossing Mat (PER-AC-70075-XX)
A4 Picot Foam (GRO-AC-40625-XX)
Groovi Plate Starter Kit (GRO-SK-40571-XX)
Groovi Border Plate Mate (GRO-MA-40348-13)
Border Pattern Grid Diagonal No. 1 (GRO-GG-40354-14)
Diagonal Basic Piercing Grid (GRO-GG-40383-14)
Pergamano Bold 1-needle perforating tool (PER-TO-70028-XX)
Pergamano Bold 2-needle perforating tool (PER-TO-70279-XX)
Pergamano Fine 2-needle perforating tool (PER-TO-70037-XX)
Pergamano scissors exclusive (PER-TO-70040-XX)
Pergamano 0.5mm Stylus (PER-TO-70010-XX)
Pergamano 1mm ball tool (PER-TO-70012-XX)
Pergamano 1.5mm ball tool (PER-TO-70004-XX)
Pergamano 3mm ball tool (PER-TO-70005-XX)
Pergamano 4.5mm ball tool (PER-TO-70015-XX)
Pergamano 2mm Star tool (PER-TO-70006-XX)
Pergamano Shader tool (PER-TO-70002-XX)
Pergamano mapping pen (PER-TO-70039-XX)
Perga Glitter (PER-AC-70252-XX)
Perga Liners (PER-CO-70063-XX)
Pergamano Dorso oil (PER-CO-70066-XX)
Perga Colour Exclusive (PER-CO-70060-XX)
Groovi Guard (GRO-AC-40345-XX)
Groovi Sticker Tabs (GRO-AC-40437-XX)

The Grid

This Border Pattern Grid comprises seven basic patterns.

These pattern grids can be used to emboss or perforate.
Emboss from the back and perforate from the front.

This book will also show you how to use these patterns to picot cut your perforations to make beautiful and intricate cut outs.

Perforated & Embossed

Here we see each of the seven patterns either embossed or perforated along a straight line, just as they come on the pattern grid.
You can also combine embossing and perforating to produce beautiful gridwork.
See instructions below and overleaf.
If you plan to perforate and emboss, it is good practice to wipe the front and back of your parchment with a tumble dryer sheet before you begin.

Perforating & Embossing

COMBINED

1. If starting with embossing

a. Attach parchment onto the pattern grid, back facing up.
b. Emboss pattern with No. 2 ball tool from Groovi Starter Kit, or 1.5mm Pergamano ball tool.
c. Remove from grid.
d. Turn parchment over (front), line up embossed dots on diagonal basic grid & attach.
e. Perforate design between embossed dots using 1-needle bold tool.

2. If starting with perforating

a. Attach parchment onto pattern grid, front facing up.
b. Perforate pattern with 1-needle bold tool.
c. Remove from grid.
d. Turn parchment over (back facing up), line up perforated holes on diagonal basic grid and attach.
e. Emboss the design between the perforated holes, again using the No. 2 or the 1.5mm ball tool.

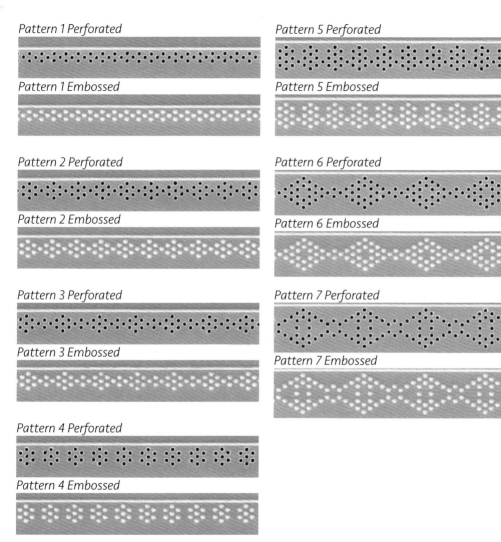

Pattern 1 Perforated

Pattern 1 Embossed

Pattern 2 Perforated

Pattern 2 Embossed

Pattern 3 Perforated

Pattern 3 Embossed

Pattern 4 Perforated

Pattern 4 Embossed

Pattern 5 Perforated

Pattern 5 Embossed

Pattern 6 Perforated

Pattern 6 Embossed

Pattern 7 Perforated

Pattern 7 Embossed

7

Picot Cutting a Line

One of the most important skills to learn when mastering the art of parchment craft is cutting. A good cut is all about cutting the connections between each perforation, to ensure a neat, even picot point. For the purpose of this book we are going to concentrate on perforations made with the aid of a Groovi Grid.

● *Perforation*　● *Cut line*

1. Place your parchment on a Straight Basic Grid and secure with Groovi Tabs to stop the parchment from sliding around. Now you are ready to perforate. Don't forget to perforate on top of a perforating mat to protect your work surface.

2. Perforate a straight line using a Straight Basic Grid.

3. When you have finished perforating you can start cutting your picot edge. During cutting you need to make sure that the waste parchment i.e. the parchment that you are cutting away, is always positioned underneath the blades of your scissors when the points are inserted into the perforations.

4. Hold the scissors with the curved end pointing downward. Put your right index finger in the left hole of the scissors and your middle finger in the right hole of the scissors. Brace your thumb against the outside of the left hole of the scissors. If you are left-handed place the index finger of your left hand in the right hole of the scissors and the middle finger in the left hole. Holding your scissors in this way may feel a little alien at first, but this is the conventional and most used way. There are numerous other ways, too many to mention, but try and find the most comfortable way that suits you. You could also try using the scissors with the curved end pointing upwards, whichever gives you the best results.

5. Now insert the points of the scissors (not too deeply) into the two perforations that are nearest to you.

6. Next, tilt the scissors down toward the paper as much as possible without removing the tips from the perforations. The scissors should be almost parallel to the paper.

7. Start the cutting motion and cut the connection between the perforations, tilting your hand and the scissors slightly towards you as you snip. You will hear a snapping noise each time you cut. A small point will be created between the perforations after each cut. Now move along the line of holes cutting as you go.

Picot Cutting a Cross

1. Place your parchment on a Straight Basic Border Grid No 1 and secure with Groovi Tabs to stop the parchment from sliding around. Now perforate the first two lines of the grid which will give you line of clusters of four perforations (much like the diagram across). Don't forget to perforate on top of a perforating mat to protect your work surface.

2. In the diagram across we have numbered the holes of the perforation so you can follow the rotations you will need to perform to achieve the cross technique. Now place the points of your scissors into perforations 1 and 2. Lower your scissors so that it is almost parallel to the parchment paper. Now make your first cut, tilting your scissors very slightly towards you as you do so. This should form a neat point known as a picot.

3. Turn your parchment a quarter turn to the left so that holes 2 and 3 are uppermost and repeat the cutting process.

4. Turn the parchment a quarter turn to the left again, so that holes 3 and 4 are uppermost and cut as before.

5. Turn the parchment for the last time so that holes 4 and 1 are now uppermost, and make your final cut. At this stage the centre should fall out leaving a neat cross shape.

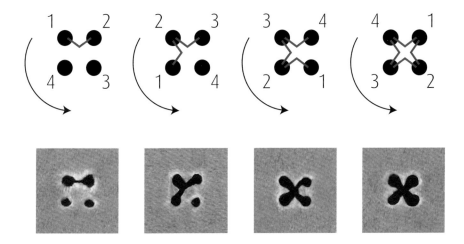

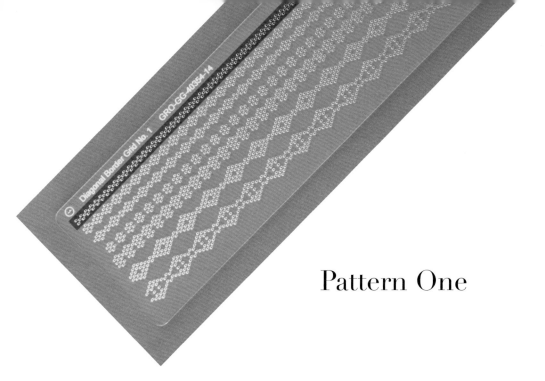

Pattern One

13

Pattern One - Perforated, Embossed & Cut

A QUICK HOW-TO USING PATTERN 1

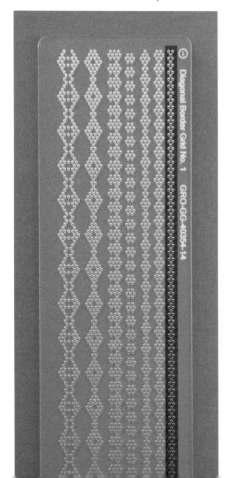

Example 1a

1. Emboss the pattern as shown (emboss five, skip four).

2. Turn the Parchment over, align the dots on the border and perforate between the embossed dots.

3. Turn the parchment to the front and picot cut.

Example 1b

1. Perforate the pattern as shown (perforate five, skip four).

2. Turn the Parchment over, align the holes on the border and emboss between the perforated holes.

3. Turn the parchment to the front and picot cut.

Example 1c

1. Emboss the pattern.

2. Turn the Parchment over. Then over the Basic Diagonal Border Grid, perforate two lines above the embossed dots.

3. Turn the parchment to the front and picot cut between the perforations..

The best
things
in life
are free

The Best Things In Life

Ingredients

Groovi Grids: *Diagonal Border Pattern Grid No.1, Diagonal Basic Border Piercing Grid.*
Plate Mates: *Alphabet A5², Art Deco Alphabet Border.*
Groovi A5² Plates: *Nested Squares, Butterflies with Words, Leafy Frame.*

To Make

1. Emboss the largest square and create 3 panels on the left.

2. Emboss the rest of the designs on the right of the panels. The butterfly is a 3D element so emboss the large butterfly on blue parchment and the medium one on regular parchment.

3. On the main piece, use Perga Liner B pencils and blend with Dorso oil to add colour to the tree trunk, branches, around the words and alternate panels. Colour the leaves with Perga Colour Exclusives.

4. Emboss and perforate the border pattern 1a in the 3 panels and outside the main card. Picot cut between the perforations.

5. Add whitework to the leaves on the butterfly wings using a small shader tool.

6. On the back, emboss dots around the butterflies wings using the basic diagonal grid and from the front perforate within the wings. Using the bold 2-needle perforating tool, perforate outside the butterfly wings and picot cut between the perforations.

7. Trim the piece of work to size and mount it on blue parchment, white card and black card using brads and attach to a 7" x 7" card blank. Fix the butterflies on the card using a small amount of Perga Glue.

8. Add sparkle to the butterfly using sticky ink, mapping pen and Perga glitter.

Faithful Friends Will Always

Leave Pawprints On Your Heart.

Faithful Friends

DESIGNED USING PATTERN 1

Ingredients

Groovi Grids: *Diagonal Border Pattern Grid No.1, Diagonal Basic Border Piercing Grid.*
Plate Mates: *Alphabet A5², Art Deco Alphabet Border, Numbers & Tags Inset.*
Groovi A5² Plates: *Nested Scallops Squares, Key To My Heart.*
Groovi A4² Plates: *Nested Squares Extension & Alphabet Frame.*

To Make

1. Emboss the largest double square outlines, scallops and dots and using the 3rd outside lines as guides, emboss lines to create panels on the top and bottom of the card.

2. Emboss the 'paw print' in the middle section and add the words in the panels.

3. Colour on the back using Perga Colours Exclusives.

4. From the back, emboss dots, over the fine diagonal grid, inside the circle on the heart. From the front, perforate every hole between the scroll designs on the paw print.

5. Using the bold 2-needle perforating tool, perforate in the keyhole and then picot cut.

6. Perforate and emboss the border pattern 1b above and below the paw print and perforate part of the border design in the scallops. Picot cut between all the perforations.

7. Trim the piece of work to size and mount it on purple parchment, white card and black card using brads and attach to a 7" x 7" card blank.

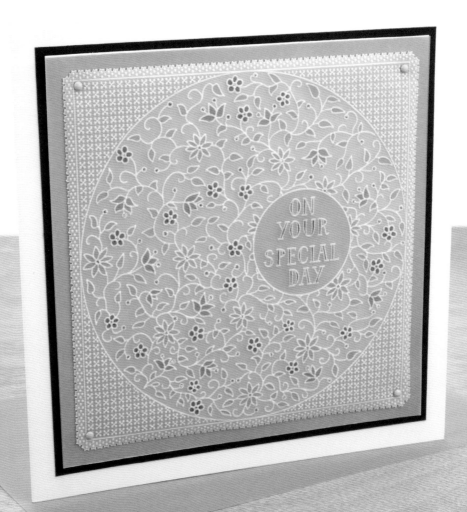

Special Day

Ingredients

Groovi Grids: *Diagonal Border Pattern Grid No.1, Diagonal Basic Border Piercing Grid. Straight Basic Grid*
Plate Mates: *Alphabet A5^2, Art Deco Alphabet Border.*
Groovi A5^2 Plates: *Nested Squares, Nested Circles, Floral Moon, Happy Birthday.*

To Make

1. Emboss the largest square and inside it the largest circle. On one side of the circle, emboss the 4th from the inside circle.

2. Emboss the rest of the designs from the plates in the circles.

3. Over the straight basic piercing grid, emboss dots in the corners between the square and the large circle. Freehand crosses between the dots using stylus (Pergamano 0.5) (See ACC-BO-30606-XX)

4. Colour on the back using Perga Colours Exclusives.

5. Emboss and perforate the border pattern 1c outside the main square and picot cut between the perforations.

6. Mount the work on blue parchment, white card and black card using brads and attach to a 7" x 7" card blank.

7. Add sparkle to the design using sticky ink, mapping pen and Perga glitter.

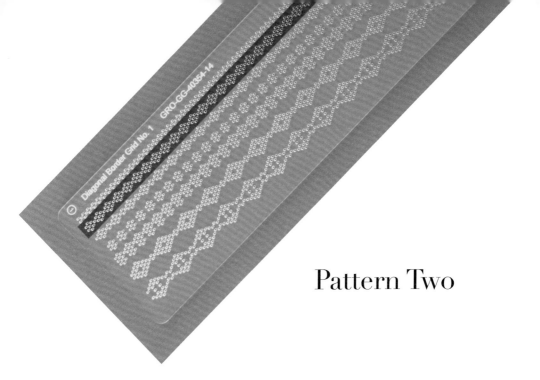

Pattern Two

Pattern Two - Perforated, Embossed & Cut

A QUICK HOW-TO USING PATTERN 2

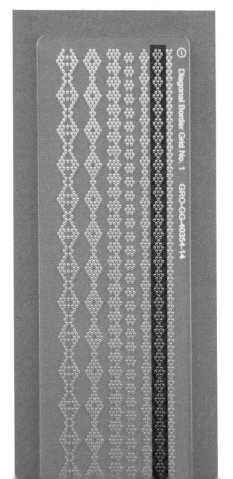

Example 2a

1. Emboss the pattern as shown.

2. Turn the Parchment over, align the dots on the border and perforate between the embossed dots.

3. Turn the parchment to the front and picot cut between the perforations.

24

Example 2b

1. Emboss the pattern as shown.

2. Turn the Parchment over, align the dots on the border and perforate between the embossed dots.

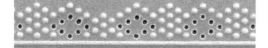

3. Turn the parchment over again to the back. Over the Basic Diagonal Border Grid, emboss extra dots around the perforations.

4. Turn the parchment to the front and picot cut between the perforations.

Example 2c

1. Emboss the pattern as shown.

2. Turn the Parchment over, align the dots on the border and perforate between the embossed dots.

3. Free hand emboss between the perforations using a 1.5mm ball tool.

4. Turn the parchment over to the front. Using the Basic Diagonal Border Grid, perforate above the embossed dots.

5. Picot cut between the perforations.

Merry Christmas

Ingredients

Groovi Grids: *Diagonal Border Pattern Grid No.1, Diagonal Basic Border Piercing Grid.*
Plate Mates: *Alphabet A5², Art Deco Alphabet Border, Calligraphy Alphabet A5.*
Groovi A5² Plates: *Nested Scallops Squares, Merry Christmas.*
Groovi A5 Plates: *Friends Dangles.*

To Make

1. Emboss the largest double square outlines, scallops and dots and the double square outlines of the 2nd from outside squares.

2. Emboss the rest of the designs from the plates inside the square.

3. Add whitework to the dangles and scallops.

4. Colour on the back using Perga Colours Exclusives.

5. Emboss and perforate the border pattern 2a between the 2 sets of squares.

6. Using the fine 2-needle perforating tool, perforate outside the scallops and picot cut between all the perforations.

7. Mount the work on purple parchment, white card and black card using brads and attach to a 7" x 7" card blank.

8. Add sparkle on the design using sticky ink, mapping pen and Perga glitter.

CONGRATULATIONS

Congratulations

Ingredients

Groovi Grids: *Diagonal Border Pattern Grid No.1, Diagonal Basic Border Piercing Grid, Straight Basic Border Piercing Grid.*
Plate Mates: *Alphabet A5², Art Deco Alphabet Border.*
Groovi A5² Plates: *Nested Squares.*
Groovi A6 Plates: *Art Nouveau Congratulations, Ballooning.*

To Make

1. Emboss the largest square and use the 3rd from outside to create panels within the square on the left and right side.

2. Emboss the rest of the designs from the plates inside the square.

3. Colour on the back using Perga Colours Exclusives for the hot air balloons and greeting. Colour the landscape and sky with Perga Liner B pencils and blend with Dorso oil.

4. Emboss and perforate the border pattern 2b in the panels. Picot cut between the perforations.

5. Over the straight basic border grid, emboss 2 rows of dots next to the border pattern and free hand emboss crosses between the dots using a stylus (Pergamano 0.5).

6. Trim the piece of work to size and mount it on blue parchment, white card and black card using brads and attach to a 7" x 7" card blank.

Noel

Ingredients

Groovi Grids: *Diagonal Border Pattern Grid No.1, Diagonal Basic Border Piercing Grid.*
Plate Mates: *Alphabet A5², Art Deco Alphabet Border.*
Groovi A5² Plates: *Nested Squares, Large Lace Netting, Small Snowflakes.*
Groovi A6 Plates: *Noel Framer.*

To Make

1. Emboss the largest 2 squares and the rest of the designs from the plates in the square.

2. Between the 2 square outlines, emboss dots using pattern 2 on the Diagonal Pattern Border Grid. Using the diagonal basic grid, emboss dots within the letters.

3. Add whitework to the large star and randomly emboss using the small star tool in the letter 'O'. On a couple of the star tool embossed stars, emboss lines extending out so they look like sparkling stars.

4. On the back, colour the sky, snowflakes and lace netting panel with Perga Liner B pencils and blend with Dorso oil. Colour the trees using Perga Colours Exclusives and for the letters and between the square outlines use a black Micron pen.

5. Emboss and perforate the border pattern 2c outside the main square. Picot cut between the perforations.

6. Attach the work on purple parchment, white card and black card using brads and attach to a 7" x 7" card blank.

7. Add sparkle on the design using sticky ink, mapping pen and Perga glitter.

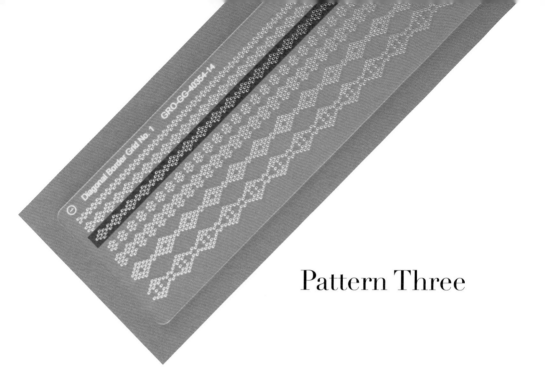

Pattern Three

Pattern Three - Perforated, Embossed & Cut

A QUICK HOW-TO USING PATTERN 3

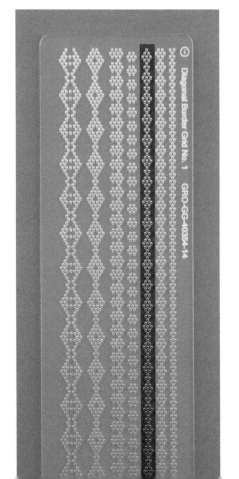

Example 3a

1. Emboss the pattern as shown.

2. Turn the Parchment over, align the dots on the border and perforate between the embossed dots.

3. Picot cut between the perforations.

Example 3b

1. Perforate the pattern as shown.

2. Turn the Parchment over, align the holes on the border and emboss between the perforated holes.

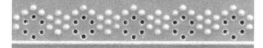

3. Turn the parchment over again to the back. Using the Basic Diagonal Border Grid, emboss extra dots above the perforations and embossed dots.

4. Turn the parchment to the front and picot cut between the perforations.

Example 3c

1. Perforate the pattern as shown.

2. Turn the parchment over to the back. Using the Basic Diagonal Border Grid, emboss extra dots between the perforations.

3. Free hand emboss between the perforations and embossed dots.

4. Turn the parchment over to the front. Using the Basic Diagonal Border Grid, perforate above the embossed dots.

5. Turn the parchment to the front and picot cut between the perforations.

Happy Birthday

Happy Birthday

DESIGNED USING PATTERN 3

Ingredients

Groovi Grids: *Diagonal Border Pattern Grid No.1.*
Plate Mates: *Alphabet A5², Art Deco Alphabet Border.*
Groovi A5² Plates: *Nested Squares, Gerbera and Butterfly, Woven Background.*
Groovi A4² Plates: *Nested Square Extension and Alphabet Frame.*

To Make

1. Emboss the largest square, followed by the gerbera in the bottom left corner. Emboss the 2nd from outside square around the flower and the rest of the designs from the plates in the square.

2. On the back, colour in the double square outlines, greeting box and flower with Perga Liner B pencils and blend with Dorso oil.

3. Emboss and perforate the border pattern 3a between the square outlines.

4. Using the bold 2-needle perforating tool, perforate in the rectangles of the woven background and outside the main square. Picot cut between all the perforations.

5. Attach the work on blue parchment, white card and black card using brads and attach to a 7" x 7" card blank.

Bumble Bees

DESIGNED USING PATTERN 3

Ingredients

Groovi Grids: *Diagonal Border Pattern Grid No.1, Diagonal Basic Border Piercing Grid.*
Plate Mates: *Alphabet A5^2, Art Deco Alphabet Border.*
Groovi A5^2 Plates: *Nested Scallops Squares, Linda's Bumblebees.*

To Make

1. Emboss the largest 2 set of squares and the 4th from the outside. Emboss the rest of the designs from the plates in the square.

2. On the back, colour the flowers, bees and leaves with Perga Colours Exclusives and the background with Perga Liner B pencils and blend with Dorso oil.

3. Perforate and emboss the border pattern 3b between the square outlines. Picot cut between all the perforations.

4. Trim the piece of work to size and mount it on purple parchment, white card and black card using brads and attach to a 7" x 7" card blank.

Remember

Ingredients

Groovi Grids: *Diagonal Border Pattern Grid No.1, Diagonal Basic Border Piercing Grid.*
Plate Mates: *Alphabet A5², Art Deco Alphabet Border.*
Groovi A5² Plates: *Nested Squares, Mountains and Hills, Poppy Field.*
Groovi Border Plates: *Dream and Miracle Word Chains.*

To Make

1. Emboss the largest 2 squares and the rest of the designs from the plates in the square.

2. Add whitework to the little flower buds and words.

3. Completely emboss pattern 2 from the diagonal pattern no 1 grid between the square outlines.

4. On the back, colour the sky and landscape with Perga Liner B pencils and blend with Dorso oil. Colour the poppy and leaves using Perga Colours Exclusives.

5. Shallow perforate the border pattern 3c outside the main square, turn over and add the whitework triangles. Turn back to the front and reperforate. Then picot cut between the perforations.

6. Mount the work on blue parchment, white card and black card using brads and attach to a 7" x 7" card blank.

7. Add sparkle on the flower buds and word using sticky ink, mapping pen and Perga glitter.

41

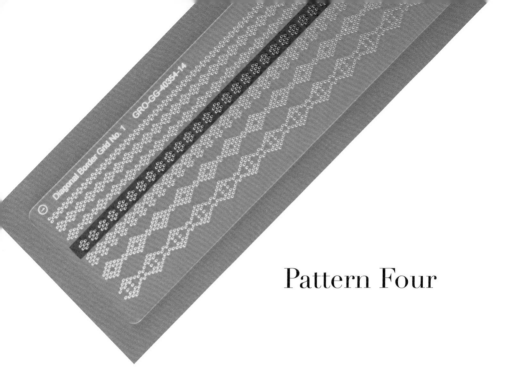

Pattern Four

Pattern Four - Perforated, Embossed & Cut

A QUICK HOW-TO USING PATTERN 4

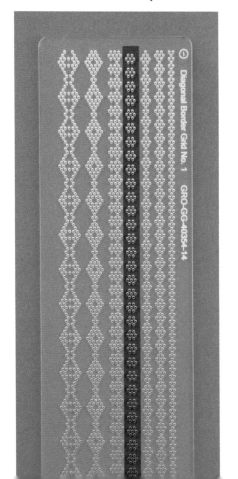

Example 4a

1. Perforate the pattern as shown.

2. Turn the Parchment over. Using the Basic Diagonal Border Grid, emboss dots between the perforations.

3. Turn the parchment to the front and picot cut between the perforations.

Example 4b

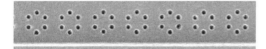

1. Perforate the pattern as shown.

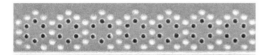

2. Turn the Parchment over. Using the Basic Diagonal Border Grid, emboss dots around the perforations.

3. Turn the parchment to the front and picot cut between the perforations.

Example 4c

1. Perforate the pattern as shown.

2. Use the Basic Diagonal Border Grid, perforate a hole between the previous perforations.

3. Turn the parchment over and free hand emboss large dots between the perforations.

4. Turn the parchment to the front and picot cut between the perforations.

Love
DESIGNED USING PATTERN 4

Ingredients

Groovi Grids: *Diagonal Border Pattern Grid No.1, Diagonal Basic Border Piercing Grid.*
Plate Mates: *Alphabet A5², Art Deco Alphabet Border.*
Groovi A5² Plates: *Nested Scallops Squares, Tina's Doodle Love Hearts* (40858),
Tina's Doodle Dove Hearts (40859).

To Make

1. Emboss the first 4 from the outside double square outlines and the scallops and dots outside the 1st and 3rd squares.

2. Emboss the rest of the designs from the plates in the square.

3. Add whitework to the bow on the rose and circles.

4. Use the Diagonal basic grid, emboss dots in the 3 dangling hearts and the heart in the word 'Love'.

5. Colour on the back with Perga Colours Exclusive.

6. Perforate and emboss the border pattern 4a between the space of the 1st and 2nd square and the 3rd and 4th square.

7. Using the fine 2-needle perforating tool, perforate outside the scallops and picot cut between all the perforations.

8. Mount the work on purple parchment, white card and black card using brads and attach to a 7" x 7" card blank.

9. Add sparkle on the flower buds and word using stick ink, mapping pen and Perga glitter.

Sending You Lots of

Hugs & Kisses.

Hugs & Kisses

DESIGNED USING PATTERN 4

Ingredients

Groovi Grids: *Diagonal Border Pattern Grid No.1, Diagonal Basic Border Piercing Grid.*
Plate Mates: *Alphabet A5², Art Deco Alphabet Border.*
Groovi A5² Plates: *Nested Squares.*
Groovi A6 Plates: *Tina's Doodle Flowers 2.*
Groovi Border Plates: *Tina's Doodle Flowers Border, New Arrival and Get Well Soon Mini Word Chains.*

To Make

1. Emboss the largest square and rest of the designs (except the words) from the plates in the square.

2. On the back, colour the panel with Perga Liner B pencils and blend with Dorso oil. Colour the petals using Perga Colours Exclusives.

3. Perforate and emboss the border pattern 4b on either side of the panel and then emboss the words on either side of the border pattern. Picot cut between all the perforations.

4. Trim the piece of work to size and mount it on blue parchment, white card and black card using brads and attach to a 7" x 7" card blank.

5. Add sparkle on the flower centres using sticky ink, mapping pen and Perga glitter.

Promise

DESIGNED USING PATTERN 4

Ingredients

Groovi Grids: *Diagonal Border Pattern Grid No.1, Diagonal Basic Border Piercing Grid.*
Plate Mates: *Alphabet A5², Art Deco Alphabet Border.*
Groovi A5² Plates: *Nested Squares, Tina's Floral Doodle Wreath.*
Groovi Border Plates: *Dream and Miracles Word Chains.*

To Make

1. Emboss the 1st and 8th squares from the outside and the rest of the designs from the plates inside the squares.

2. Colour on the back with Perga Colours Exclusives.

3. Perforate and emboss the border pattern 4c on either side of the word panel and outside the main card.

4. Using the bold 2-needle perforating tool, perforate along the remaining 3 sides inside the small square on either side of the border pattern 4c. Picot cut between all the perforations.

5. Mount the work on purple parchment, white card and black card using brads and attach to a 7" x 7" card blank.

6. Add sparkle on the flower centres using sticky ink, mapping pen and Perga glitter.

Pattern Five

Pattern Five - Perforated, Embossed & Cut

A QUICK HOW-TO USING PATTERN 5

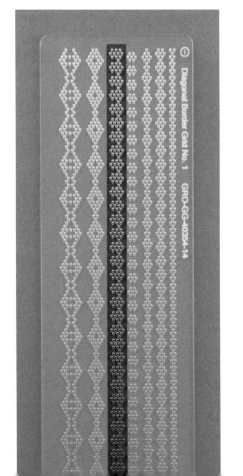

Example 5a

1. Perforate the pattern as shown.

2. Turn the Parchment over. Align the holes on the border and emboss above the perforations.

3. Free hand emboss between the perforations.

3. Turn the parchment to the front and picot cut between the perforations.

Example 5b

1. Perforate the pattern as shown.

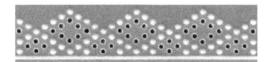

2. Turn the Parchment over. Use the Basic Diagonal Border Grid, emboss dots above and between the perforations.

3. Turn the parchment to the front and picot cut between the perforations.

Example 5c

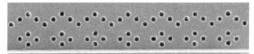

1. Perforate the pattern as shown.

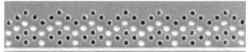

2. Turn the Parchment over. Use the Basic Diagonal Border Grid, emboss dots between the perforations.

3. Turn the parchment to the front and picot cut between the perforations.

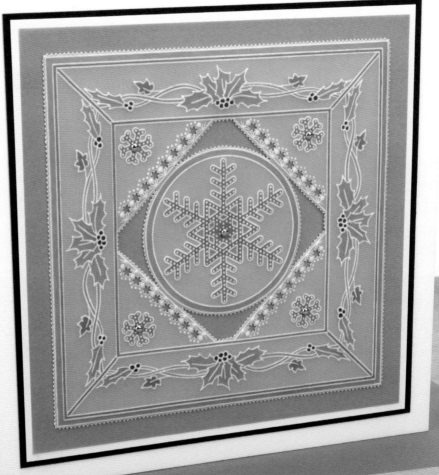

Snowflake

DESIGNED USING PATTERN 5

Ingredients

Groovi Grids: *Diagonal Border Pattern Grid No.1, Diagonal Basic Border Piercing Grid, Small Snowflakes Grid A5².*
Plate Mates: *Alphabet A5², Art Deco Alphabet Border.*
Groovi A5² Plates: *Jayne's Holly and Ivy Name Plate, Small Snowflakes Outline.*
Groovi A4² Plates: *Nested Squares Extension and Alphabet Frame, Framework Circles.*

To Make

1. Emboss the frame and the rest of the designs from the plates inside the frame.

2. When working with the snowflakes, it is best to emboss the dots first and then add the outline.

3. Colour on the back with Perga Colours Exclusives.

4. Perforate and emboss the border pattern 5a diagonally in the corners.

5. Using the bold 2-needle perforating tool, perforate the sections between the circle and the border pattern 5a and outside the main square. Picot cut between all the perforations.

6. Mount the work on blue parchment, white card and black card using brads and attach to a 7" x 7" card blank.

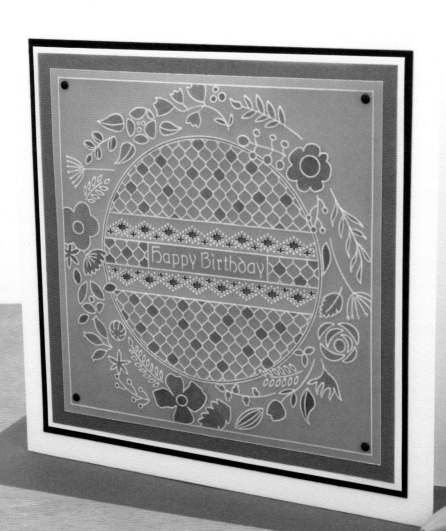

Happy Birthday

Floral Birthday

Ingredients

Groovi Grids: *Diagonal Border Pattern Grid No.1, Diagonal Basic Border Piercing Grid.*
Plate Mates: *Alphabet A5², Art Deco Alphabet Border.*
Groovi A5² Plates: *Nested Squares, Nested Scallops Circles, Butterfly Wreath, Large Lace Netting, Celtic Corners.*

To Make

1. Emboss the largest square and the 3rd double circle from the outside. Emboss the rest of the design from the plates in the square.

2. On the back, using Perga Liner B pencils, colour the lace netting sections and around the inside edges of the square and blend with Dorso oil. Colour the floral wreath and random netting sections with Perga Colours Exclusives.

3. Perforate and emboss the border pattern 5b on either side of the greeting panel and picot cut between the perforations.

4. Trim the work to size and mount it on purple parchment, white card and black card using brads and attach to a 7" x 7" card blank.

The Perfect Handbag

DESIGNED USING PATTERN 5

Ingredients

Groovi Grids: *Diagonal Border Pattern Grid No.1, Diagonal Basic Border Piercing Grid.*
Plate Mates: *Alphabet A5², Art Deco Alphabet Border.*
Groovi A5² Plates: *Nested Scallops Squares, Netting Pattern.*
Groovi Border Plates: *Handbags.*

To Make

1. Emboss the largest set of squares square and the 4th from inside set of squares.

2. Emboss the rest of the designs from the plates in the square.

3. On the back, colour between the square outlines and the handbag with Perga Colour Exclusive pens.

4. Using a 2 needle tool, perforate inside the netting pattern and picut cut between the perforations.

5. Perforate and emboss the border pattern 5c outside the main square. Picot cut between the perforations.

6. Mount the work on blue parchment, white card and black card using brads and attach to a 7" x 7" card blank.

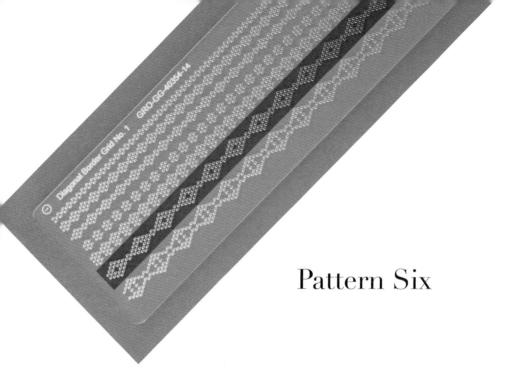

Diagonal Border Grid No. 1   GRO-GC-40354-14

Pattern Six

Pattern Six - Perforated, Embossed & Cut

A QUICK HOW-TO USING PATTERN 6

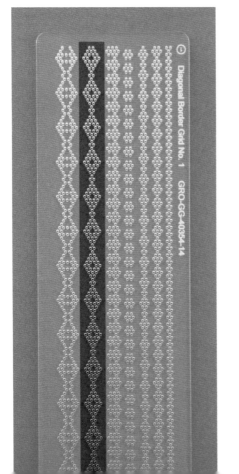

Example 6a

1. Emboss the pattern as shown.

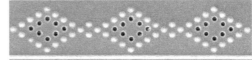

2. Turn the Parchment over. Align the dots on the border and perforate between the embossed dots.

3. Turn the parchment to the front and picot cut between the perforations.

Example 6b

1. Perforate the pattern as shown.

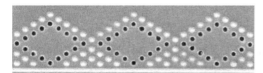

2. Turn the Parchment over. Use the Basic Diagonal Border Grid, emboss dots above and below the perforations.

3. Turn the parchment to the front and picot cut between the perforations.

Example 6c

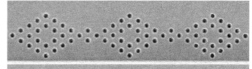

1. Perforate the pattern as shown.

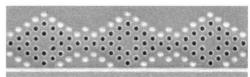

2. Turn the Parchment over. Use the Basic Diagonal Border Grid, emboss dots above and below the perforations.

3. Free hand emboss between the perforations as shown.

3. Turn the parchment to the front and picot cut between the perforations.

Daisies

Ingredients

Groovi Grids: *Diagonal Border Pattern Grid No.1, Diagonal Basic Border Piercing Grid.*
Plate Mates: *Alphabet A5², Art Deco Alphabet Border.*
Groovi A5² Plates: *Nested Scallops Circles, Nested Squares.*
Groovi A6² Plates: *Daisies.*

To Make

1. Emboss the largest square from the nested squares plate and the 3rd from outside set of circles, scallops and dots from the nested circles plates. Emboss the daisy design in the circle.

2. Add whitework to the daisy design.

3. On the back, colour the daisy design with Perga Colours Exclusive. Colour the space between the square and the scallops with Perga Liner B pencils and blend with Dorso oil.

4. Emboss and perforate the border pattern 6a outside diagonally in the 4 corners of the square.

5. Using the bold 2-needle perforating tool perforate inside the scallops and outside the main square. Picot cut between all the perforations.

6. Mount the work on purple parchment, white card and black card using brads and attach to a 7" x 7" card blank.

Wishing You a

Happy Birthday

Wishing You A Happy Birthday

DESIGNED USING PATTERN 6

Ingredients

Groovi Grids: *Diagonal Border Pattern Grid No.1, Diagonal Basic Border Piercing Grid.*
Plate Mates: *Alphabet A5², Art Deco Alphabet Border.*
Groovi A5² Plates: *Nested Squares.*
Groovi A4² Plates: *Nested Squares Extension and Alphabet Frame,*
Tina's Henna Corners 1.

To Make

1. Emboss the 2nd and 3rd squares from the outside and the rest of the designs from the plates in the square.

2. Use the diagonal basic grid, emboss dots in the top left corner between the henna design.

3. Completely emboss pattern 4 from the diagonal pattern no.1 grid between the diagonal outlines in the top left corner and the square frame.

4. On the back, colour with Perga Liner B pencils the borders and the large sections of the henna designs and blend with Dorso oil. Colour the small elements with Perga Colours Exclusives.

5. Perforate and emboss the border pattern 6b outside outside the main square and picot cut between all the perforations.

6. Trim the work to size and mount it on blue parchment, white card and black card using brads and attach to a 7" x 7" card blank.

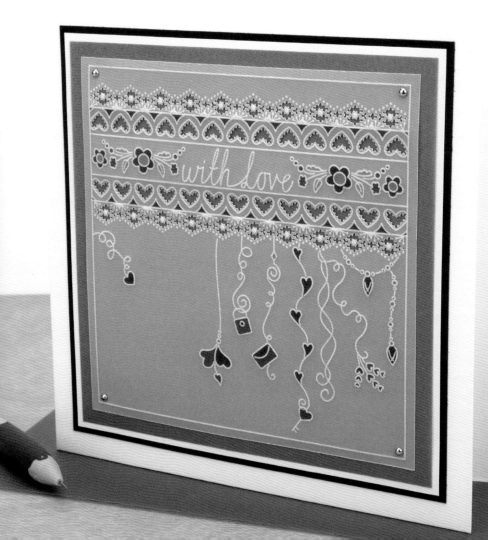

With Love

Ingredients

Groovi Grids: *Diagonal Border Pattern Grid No.1, Diagonal Basic Border Piercing Grid.*
Plate Mates: *Alphabet A5², Art Deco Alphabet Border.*
Groovi A5² Plates: *Nested Squares.*
Groovi A5 Plates: *Love Dangles.*
Groovi Border Plates: *Tina's Doodle Hearts 1, Tina's Floral Doodle, Best Wishes Line Sentiment.*

To Make

1. Emboss the largest square and use the 4th, 6th, 9th, and 11th squares as guides for where to put the panels. Emboss the rest of the designs (not the dangles) from the plates inside the panels.

2. On the back, colour the heart panels with Perga Liner B pencils and blend with Dorso oil.

3. Perforate and emboss the border pattern 6c above and below the border heart designs.

4. Emboss the dangles and colour the elements in the greeting panel and the dangles using Perga Colours Exclusive.

5. Using the bold 2-needle perforating tool perforate inside hearts. Picot cut between all the perforations.

6. Trim the work to size and mount it on purple parchment, white card and black card using brads and attach to a 7" x 7" card blank.

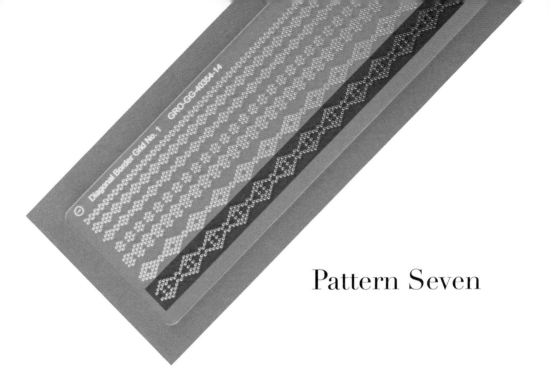

Pattern Seven

Pattern Seven - Perforated, Embossed & Cut

A QUICK HOW-TO USING PATTERN 7

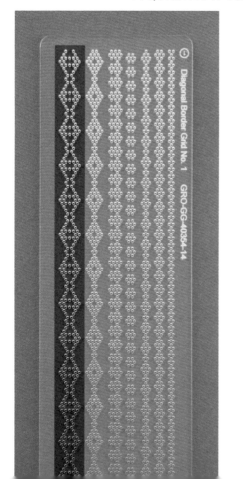

Example 7a

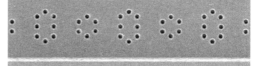

1. Perforate the pattern as shown.

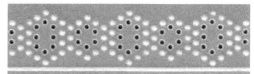

2. Turn the Parchment over. Use the Basic Diagonal Border Grid, emboss dots around the perforations.

3. Turn the parchment to the front and picot cut between the perforations.

Example 7b

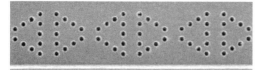

1. Perforate the pattern as shown.

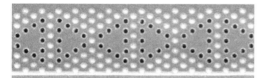

2. Turn the Parchment over. Use the Basic Diagonal Border Grid, emboss dots around the perforations.

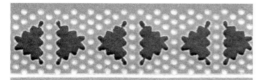

3. Turn the parchment to the front and picot cut between the perforations.

Example 7c

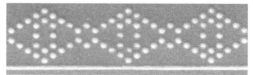

1. Emboss the pattern as shown.

2. Free hand emboss between the embossed dots using a 0.5mm ball tool.

3. Turn the Parchment over. Use the Basic Diagonal Border Grid, perforate above and between the embossed dots.

4. Picot cut between the perforations.

Your
SPeCial
Day

Your Special Day

DESIGNED USING PATTERN 7

Ingredients

Groovi Grids: *Diagonal Border Pattern Grid No.1, Diagonal Basic Border Piercing Grid.*
Plate Mates: *Alphabet A5², Art Deco Alphabet Border.*
Groovi A5² Plates: *Nested Squares, Nested Scallops Circles, Jayne's Trumpet Lilies, Jayne's Fuchsias Name Plate.*
Groovi Border Plates: *Merry Christmas and Birthday Mini Word Chains.*

To Make

1. Emboss the 1st, 3rd and 5th squares from the outside and add diagonal lines across the squares to create a frame. Emboss the rest of the designs from the plates in the square.

2. On the back, colour with Perga Liner B pencils and blend with Dorso oil.

3. Perforate and emboss the border pattern 7a between the alternate frames and picot cut between all the perforations.

4. Trim the work to size and mount it on blue parchment, white card and black card using brads and attach to a 7" x 7" card blank.

Forever Friends

Ingredients

Groovi Grids: *Diagonal Border Pattern Grid No.1, Diagonal Basic Border Piercing Grid.*
Plate Mates: *Alphabet A5², Art Deco Alphabet Border.*
Groovi A5² Plates: *Nested Scallops Squares, Sprig Background.*
Groovi Border Plates: *Gratitude and Sending Hugs Word Chains.*

To Make

1. Emboss the largest set of squares and scallops and the rest of the designs from the plates in the square.

2. On the back, colour the sprig and greeting panels with Perga Liner B pencils and blend with Dorso oil. Colour the leaves, words and between the set of square outlines with Perga Colours Exclusives.

3. Emboss part of pattern 1 from the diagonal pattern no1 grid in the scallops, moving the parchment so the design fits inside each scallop.

4. Perforate and emboss the border pattern 7b in the panels above and below the words.

5. Using the fine 2-needle perforating tool perforate outside the scallops. Picot cut between all the perforations.

6. Mount the work on purple parchment, white card and black card using brads and attach to a 7" x 7" card blank.

New Home

Ingredients

Groovi Grids: *Diagonal Border Pattern Grid No.1, Diagonal Basic Border Piercing Grid.*
Plate Mates: *Alphabet A5², Art Deco Alphabet Border.*
Groovi A5² Plates: *Nested Scallops Squares, Nested Squares.*
Groovi A6² Plates: *Wee Houses and Lamp Posts, Wee Shops and Tree, Alphabet Uppercase.*
Groovi Border Plates: *Lawn Art Nouveau.*

To Make

1. Emboss the 2nd from the outside square from the nested squares plate and the 4th from the inside set of squares from the nested scallops squares plate. Emboss the rest of the designs from the plates in the squares.

2. Add whitework to the corner flower petals using a small shader tool.

3. On the back, colour the section between the main square and the inside square with Perga Liner B pencils and blend with Dorso oil. Colour the house, lamp posts, flower centres and between the double square outlines with Perga Colours Exclusives.

4. Use the diagonal basic grid, emboss dots in the corner designs.

5. Emboss and perforate the border pattern 7c outside the main square and picot cut between all the perforations.

6. Mount the work on blue parchment, white card and black card using brads and attach to a 7" x 7" card blank.

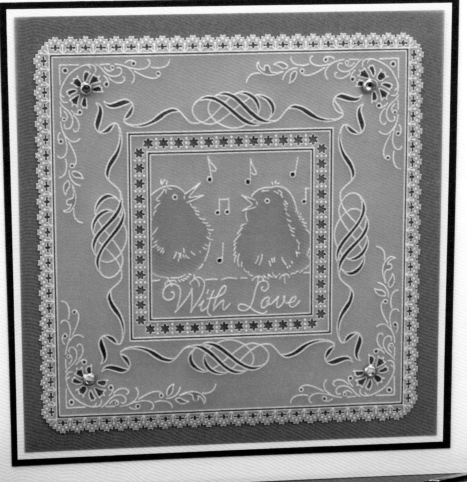

The **Big** Project

Bird Song

Now that we have studied this clever diagonal pattern plate, let's put our knowledge into practice. By picot cutting our perforated pattens to create beautiful, lacy borders and frames, we can elevate our parchment crafting to the next level.

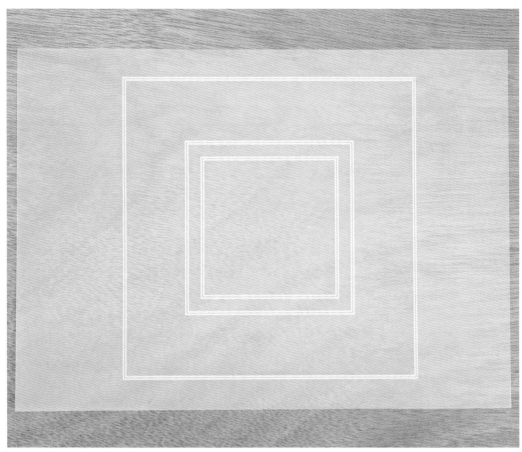

1. From the Nested Scallops Squares Groovi plate and using the No1 Groovi embossing tool (or Pergamano 1mm), emboss the largest set of squares and from the inside the 4th and 5th set of squares.

2. From the Brads Corners 2 border plate, emboss the design in the corners.

3. From the Art Deco Alphabet border plate, emboss the ribbon design around the middle square.

4. From the We Wish You a Merry Christmas plate, emboss the robins and music notes in the little square.

5. From the occasions border plate emboss the greeting under the robins.

6. On the back, colour inside the small square and in the corners of the main square with Perga Liners and blend with Dorso oil. Colour the birds in the same way.

7. On the back, colour the corner designs and ribbons with Perga Colours Exclusive.

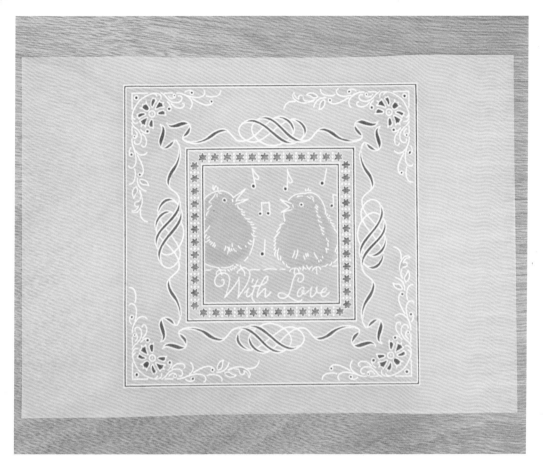

8. Perforate and emboss the border pattern 4a in the between the small square and middle square. Picot cut between all the perforations.

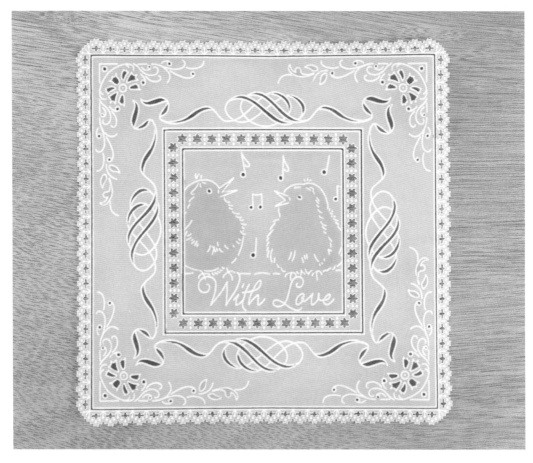

9. Perforate and emboss the border pattern 2c outside the main square. Picot cut between all the perforations.

To Finish: Mount the work on purple parchment, white card and black card using brads and attach to a 7" x 7" card blank.

93

Index Of Groovi Plates Used

A4 Square Plates:

Nested Square Extension - GRO-WO-40538-15
Framework Circles - GRO-PA-40722-15
Tina's Henna Corners 1 - GRO-FL-40662-15

A5 Square Pates:

Nested Squares - GRO-PA-40037-03
Butterflies with Words - GRO-AN-40229-03
Numbers & Tags Inset - GRO-WO-40133-11
Nested Scallops Squares - GRO-PA-40557-03
Key to My Heart - GRO-LO-40536-03
Nested Circles - GRO-PA-40048-03
Floral Moon - GRO-FL-40446-03
Happy Birthday - GRO-WO-40276-03
Merry Christmas - GRO-WO-40275-03
Large Lace Netting - GRO-PA-40339-03
Small Snowflakes - GRO-WI-40725-03
Gerbera & Butterfly - GRO-FL-40753-03
Linda's Butterflies - GRO-AN-40816-03
Mountains & Hills - GRO-LA-40007-03
Poppy Field - GRO-FL-40075-03
Tina's Doodle Love Hearts - GRO-LO-40858-03
Tina's Doodle Dove Hearts - GRO-LO-40859-03
Tina's Floral Doodle Wreath - GRO-FL-40830-03
Jayne's Holly & Ivy Name Plate - GRO-FL-40386-03
Butterfly Wreath - GRO-FL-40005-03
Celtic Corners - GRO-PA-40851-03
Jayne's Trumpet Lillies - GRO-FL-40321-03
Jaybnes Fuchsias Name Plate - GRO-FL-40394-03
Sprig Background - GRO-FL-40008-03
Wish You A Merry Christmas - GRO-CH-40742-03

A5 Plates:

Friends Dangles - GRO-WO-40838-04
Love Dangles - GRO-WO-40839-04

A6 Square Plates:

A New Arrival - GRO-CN-40291-01
Daisies - GRO-FL-40164-01
Wee Houses & Lamp Post - GRO-HO-40332-01
Wee Shops & Tree - GRO-HO-40331-01
Alphabet Uppercase - GRO-WO-40225-01

A6 Plates:

Art Nouveau Congratulations - GRO-WO-40836-02
Ballooning - GRO-TV-40665-02
Noel Framer - GRO-WO-40599-02
Tina's Doodle Flowers 2 - GRO-FL-40757-02

Border Plates:

Dream & Miracle Word Chains - GRO-WO-40567-09
Tina's Doodle Flower Border - GRO-PA-40848-09
Get Well Soon Mini Word Chains - GRO-WO-40891-09
Handbags - GRO-FA-40498-09
Best Wishes Line Sentiments - GRO-WO-40105-09
Merry Christmas & Birthday Mini Word Chains -
GRO-WO-40888-09
Gratitude & Sending Hugs Word Chains
GRO-WO-40564-09
Lawn - Art Nouveau - GRO-PE-40110-09
Brad Corners 2 - GRO-CO-40759-09
Occasions - GRO-WO-40060-09